THE HOUSE NOT RIGHT IN THE HEAD

A. D. FOOTE

Dundee
Blind Serpent
1986

First published by Blind Serpent
65 Magdalen Yard Road, Dundee. DD2 1AL

ISBN 0 9511678 0 4

The publisher acknowledges subsidy from the Scottish Arts Council
towards the publication of this volume.

Acknowledgements are due to the Editors
of the following publications:

Blind Serpent, Gallimaufry,
Seagate II, and Words Magazine

Cover illustration by Walter McLean

PREFACE

Although sometimes bleak, the experience and vision that inform A. D. Foote's poems testify to life's common and affirmative design, that of sickness and recovery. It is a story on which Foote's perspectives are ironic and lucid; as a result, he avoids both self-aggrandizing euphoria and cheap optimism.

For example, in "The Visionary", he contrasts an experience of so-called insanity with its aftermath during alleged normality, saying,

> For how can I tell
> Whether I was deluded, seeing what I saw,
> Or seeing nothing now, am deluded the more?

Poetry has been chewing on that question for hundreds of years. No doubt its mastication will continue for hundreds more.

I get the impression from the feel of Foote's poetry that he has found himself able to see his life and opinions in stark clarity and that he has enjoyed (if that is the word) opportunities to see beyond his life. Therefore he questions the status of reality. In "Delusions of Grandeur" a well-travelled fantasist is 'cured' of his imaginary voyaging, and, made 'better' by therapy, ends up working in a jute mill in Dundee. Which of his realities is preferable? The poem is a good example of the wry pleasures to be found in Foote's writing, over a wider range of experience, the whole adding up to a collection that is firmly and passionately subjective.

Douglas Dunn

CONTENTS

Part One: Gulls on a Hospital Roof

	Page
Morningside	6
Un Mauvais Quart D'Heure	7
Chronics	7
The Introvert	8
Gulls on a Hospital Roof	8
Delusions of Grandeur	9
The Scholar	10
Pay Parade	11
The Temperate Aquarium	12
Ornithomancy	12
The Visionary	13
The House Not Right in the Head	14

Part Two: The Hunters with Their Guns

Mid-Craigie	16
After New Year	16
After Ecclesiastes	17
The Emigré	18
Holiday Week in Fife	19
The Initiate	20
Reading the Mail	21
Inheritors	22
The Anchoress	23

Part Three: Relics

Relics	25
The Volapükists	26
Three Dreams:	
1. The Husband's Dream	27
2. The Wife's Dream	28
3. The Child's Dream	28
An Arts Degree	29
V-J Day	30
Soft Corn	31
Programmer	32
September	33
La Grand' Place, Brussels	34
Bachelor	35
La Baule in Autumn	36

PART ONE

Gulls on a Hospital Roof

MORNINGSIDE

(Royal Edinburgh Hospital)

An hour by train over the Two Bridges,
And then a bus trip through the city
And I saw it, a plain monastic building
Whose windows all looked inwards to a cloister
Set in a sunken Italian garden.
After booking in on the ground floor
I went up the two flights of stairs
And met a man meditatively playing the guitar
Who asked me if I had read the Bhagavad-Gita.
There were squirrels in the gardens
And a 'Sunday Mirror' lying
Incongruously unattended on the window-seat.
They then brought us our meal, cold potatoes
Followed by ice-cream
Rolled along corridors on a trolley
Which the patients referred to as 'the barry'.
And an old man they called Donald
Chattered all night in the next bed
About his youth, his girl-friend, and Charlotte Square.
The next day was Saturday
And nothing to do all day
But to arrange one's toothbrush on the locker
Next the bed, and contemplate the sky through the skylight,
I thought of Dutch double consonants,
And verbal suffixes in Turkish,
And of everything but my predicament,
And wandered round the empty corridors
Trying at the doors of frosted glass.

UN MAUVAIS QUART D' HEURE

The evening before, they moved him into a side-room;
The walls no longer made their mouths at him,
And the fitted carpets, bright yellow,
Resounded with no sonorous jackboots.
He briefly pondered
Whether to hang himself in the toilet
With a section of the window-cord,
Or die more subtly, by holding his breath.
Then, at four in the morning, he awoke;
That was it; they were strangling him again
With dreams sent out on the etheric wavelength,
When, all at once, he noticed
Cloud-draped, the sunrise dawn
With the breathless hush of a catafalque.

CHRONICS

However much the healing fingers probe
They cannot reach the distant buried spring
Concealed within these hearts, however loud
The stones re-echo here, they cannot speak
Of torments undergone in days gone by.
Those who survived now sit in docile rows
For each night's entertainment, roam the halls
Of their dead selves, scattering the shards

Indifferent alike to shower and sun.
Like unloved ghosts, they haunt a fixed terrain
But have no favourite or private spaces

And shapes of terror from the muted screen
Leap to relief and blunt themselves in vain
Against these pert or adamantine faces.

THE INTROVERT

I live in a secret cave
Where no man has set foot.
From the roof hang icicles,
And on the walls, mirrors.
Like the brown leaves of the beech
I look at my thousand faces
Which never alter nor grow old.

GULLS ON A HOSPITAL ROOF

Forever seeming undecided,
Immobilised,
Like stiff senators they sit
In their encumbered poses
Waiting for the heavens to open
And rain down loaves and fishes.

In this they resemble
The human sick:
Awaiting a miracle
That will set them free,
Or perhaps they are the souls
Of dead relations
Come back to harass the living.

Someone throws a crust:
The hulks launch into frenzied
Life, brawl and bicker
Till, one by one, they fall
Exhausted
Once more into coma.

DELUSIONS OF GRANDEUR

'Oh, yes, I've been to Spitzbergen,' he said,
'Built myself a hut from the ship's timbers
With my bare hands:
We lived on meat from a whale's carcass
Stranded on the shore.'

Next day I happened to mention Tenerife.
He'd been there as well.
'The native girls wear roses behind their ears
That they give to any stranger
They want to spend the night with.'

When he had been a month on the ward
It came out
He had never even been in Dundee
Except for a night he spent in the police-cell
On the way to hospital.

Then when he did go
He lost his way between City Square and the bus-stop
And had to be brought back
In an ambulance.

'It's not at all like Siberia,' he ruefully confided,
'There you can follow the trails the reindeer make
For miles across the tundra
Until you reach your base.'

It would be satisfying to relate
That he ended by pushing off
To China or the Antarctic;
But in fact he, strangely, got better
And now works in a jute-mill
Off the Perth Road.

THE SCHOLAR

'Why study Arabic?' I asked him.
'Why study anything at all?' he said,
'When we have no prospect of ever
Leaving this place of gloom and shadow,
No hope of ever emerging
As men, in our own right...'

So nightly he proceeds
Painfully from *alif* to *yaw*,
Tracing a path within his mind
Where only rocks and stones abound.
I sometimes wish the swallow's flaunting wings
Could warm him and transform him,
But nothing in nature manages
To rouse a flicker of interest.
In this he is like so many
Who labour only to be left with
No answer to the riddle
Of the soul's emptiness;
Who year after year come up with
The same hoary old clichés,
As the earth comes up with
Perennial weeds.
But even weeds are a kind of life
And better than nothing at all
For these, on whose chance of freedom
The key has finally turned.

PAY PARADE

Converting pence into dollars or Finnish marks,
I wonder cynically what I would have in real
Terms if I lived in Houston or Helsinki:
Much more, at least enough for a decent meal

In town ... 'What more do you want?' the nurse cries.
'A roof over your head, no laundry bills,
No gas or electricity to pay for ... !'
I want the silence of the ancient hills

And a place in the sun, something to live for,
Not just this passive existence from hand to mouth
On bread and water, with half-crazy companions ...
As Keats said, 'A beaker full of the warm South'

But Keats died of tuberculosis in Italy
And madhouses were Bedlam in his day;
Then I go out into the open air, and the sky
Is covered with little specks of blue and grey

Like a pigeon's plumage, and the breeze blows up
Over the Carse with the smell of new-mown hay,
And I realise that money cannot buy contentment
And Heaven gives more than man can take away.

THE TEMPERATE AQUARIUM

In the bedroom not far from my own,
A friend has started a temperate aquarium.
He has three goldfish; two have died,
Of bladder trouble, and the third is sickly.
I have recently written three poems,
Two are finished, and the third is maturing.
How long will it be before I come home
One night to find them floating on the water
Like my friend's goldfish?

ORNITHOMANCY*

or THE FOWL OF DR. FOWLIE

One day, at a loose end, in Ward Seven,
I grumbled to the parrot in the cage
That hung in the window by the television:
'I've been here, Polly, now for seven months
And still I don't get better.'

He looked me over with a rolling eye,
And then, to my intense surprise, replied:
'Less a scholar:
More a person.'

I asked for more convincing information,
But all that he would say in answer was:
'Don't THINK:
ACT!'

I've been discharged now and I'm doing fine,
And often marvel at that bird's acuity;
And as for the advice he gave me, well —
It was quicker than going to a psychiatrist
As well as wiser.

*Ornithomancy: divination by birds.

THE VISIONARY

I had a waking dream — like Gerontius or Guinevere —
Of children in African or Indian dress, walking
On lawns diaphanous as crystal
Round a palace white as marble —
In joy for the Most Great Peace,
And these were the seed that should inherit the earth
When the West was dead and done for.

And I saw the spirits of all men living, or who would ever live
Ascending and descending the stairs of Heaven,
With reincarnation a blessed fact: some were studying
To be artists and musicians, some potters
At their next birth: others remained
In Heaven to educate and encourage the rest.

I sent a message to my loved ones
Saying that I was dying, or soon to die,
And that I would await them in the anteroom of Heaven
For all this should come to pass.

And they called me insane, and shut me in an asylum,
But through its windows I heard the spirits still singing
And saw the delicate diaphanous costumes they wove
Out of their own thoughts: their presence was constantly
With me by day and by night.

And now I am sane again, I go rejoicing,
Knowing that all this must come to pass,
For how can I tell
Whether I was deluded, seeing what I saw,
Or seeing nothing now, am deluded the more?

THE HOUSE NOT RIGHT IN THE HEAD

Five years I spent in its impassive embrace,
    Sharing my bed and board
With every mad Tom, deranged Dick and hapless Harry
    In Scotia's plentiful hoard

Who scrounged my fags, made tea and bawdy jokes
    And danced on party nights
Or just remained anonymous, outside
    The aura of the lights

Thinking their own thoughts, keeping themselves
    Severely to themselves;
I never really knew them, thinking of them
    As pixies or as elves

Who sometimes threw a tantrum or went berserk:
    It wasn't my affair,
And I never seriously questioned why
    Either I or they were there

And letters from friends in England kept arriving
    Gilding my days and hours
With hopes that quickly seemed a sham, deceiving
    As artificial flowers,

And the years went by, and I learnt to acquire the poise
    Of the fir tree in the grounds
That bent its branches to the snow that piled above it
    Till the doctors on their rounds

Saw fit to give me my discharge one morning,
    And the world became more real
(The outside world with its panache and pathos)
    And I began to feel

Like a pheasant that has survived the mating season
    And now that autumn comes
Hears toiling up the road that leads to its covert
    The hunters with their guns.

PART TWO

The Hunters with Their Guns

MID-CRAIGIE

The trees they planted here six years ago
Failed to take root.
Instead, the ground sprouted
Aerosols, dog turds, cans and bottles.
The middle-aged, who still remember the slums
Now older, pass by, hunch-backed,
Looking for something on the ground,

Something of value they lost long ago,
Before these fields were built upon.
Only the ever-living children shout and leap
At their unending play,

Growing up straight in a different world.

AFTER NEW YEAR

One by one the old places
                become habitable again,
Shops reopen, showing signs of wear and tear.
So (days later) do libraries.
                        The scholar
Has a glorious excuse to do
                nothing in public. The police,
Tired of waiting for someone to commit a crime,
Tow innocent cars to secret destinations.

This is the time when we know
                everything will come to pass;
In spring or summer, we are not quite sure.
All is predictable, even Death; and we accept
Suffering like falling shares or a freak tornado.

AFTER ECCLESIASTES

There is a time for action
(The swift tattle of the squash racket)
There is a time for words
Orotund and lugubrious:
There is a time for Zenny silence
Sitting, watching the cloud-drift,
And there is a time to be dissolute.

But this time, time broke down
When I awoke after nightmare
And the sun rose at 3 a.m.
And I tiptoed round the house
So as not to wake the other occupants
With fear in the whites of my eyes
As if it were Armageddon.

Man is a maker of time:
Egg-boiling time, seduction-time,
          professional-success-time
Like no animal:

I make time for poetry-writing
Which takes on average, thirty odd years
And a few moments
And maybe eternity.

THE EMIGRÉ

Here where the trellis on the south-facing wall
Supports a few decayed rose-plants,
He sits on a bench, hoping that today
Someone will bring him a letter.

In the street the children are playing transistors
In the innocence of their lust,
But all the Herzian waves that travel
Across the continents cannot efface the fact
That he alone is lonely and unwanted.

The tides have left him, like a jagged wreck,
Have flowed elsewhere, taking their gaiety and horseplay.
He stays behind, encrusted in the sand,
Like a solitary starfish
Fixing the heavens with its baleful eye.

HOLIDAY WEEK IN FIFE

The lawn-mower moves up and down rhythmically,
Spurting minuscule rivulets of grass.
Day and night the tides caress the sea wall,
Where, listlessly, the shadows of sea-gulls pass.

The post van drops off mail for the distant hamlet;
The herring fleets head landward and unload.
A startled sheep from the golf course scatters pellets
Of delicate dung on the macadamed road.

Summer comes tardily: cars replete with tourists
Fill up their tanks, and workers from Dundee
Tired with watching the gaunt looms in jute mills,
Watch sunlight weave a pattern of joy on the sea.

Under the turf the souls of Pictish warlords
And Irish saints who blazoned the unknown
(Now only names to tantalise the schoolchild)
Sleep in their coffins of impassive stone.

THE INITIATE

As a boy he collected tadpoles:
Fluorescent bodies swimming around a jar
Brought from some stinking brook
On the outskirts of the town.

And later, in the Sixth,
He collected Latin phrases:
Odi et amo: he loved to watch them
Shimmer and reflect the light.

And when his one true love
Appeared in his life,
It was because she reminded him
Of those diviner moments
Of boyish bliss.

Now he is old, he has only
His memories left,
But sometimes even these
Will flower intolerably, recalling
Tadpoles in a jar, a woman's voice,
Or the grandeur that was Rome.

READING THE MAIL

Six a.m. and it's chatterbox time:
WPC Richardson
Quotes a stolen car number
To H.Q. Roger.
A blind man's cane
Tapping in the street.
All's quiet,
If not clean, on Sidlaw side.
Better make a trip and see some action:
How about that?
Somewhere in Carpathian wastes
A carcass of steel affronts the sky:
Missile launcher or transmitter?
Those Russkis again
With punk rock from Lenin's tomb.
Nearby, the Yanks debate endlessly
What Reagan did or did not say.
Six-ten: London wakes up
With news of oil futures and a hangover from Ulster.
The jamming gets louder:
A pissed evangelist from Geneva
Promises damnation to the unbaptised:
I feel a headache coming on.
Switch off. Bliss.
Over my head a lucid moon composes
Anthems of silence from Cloud City.

Reading the mail: overhearing conversation
Make a trip: change channels
Cloud City: Heaven

INHERITORS

My mother bequeathed me
Her Bachelor's degree, her Bible
Set in diamond point
And a Lallans tale about
Two Musselburgh fishwives.

When Hitler's war broke out
We came north to Galloway
And searched in vain for a house.
Big girls climbed tall trees,
And shouted 'Imbecile!' at one another.
Old men in the Square
Said it couldn't last six weeks.

My father called us 'gomerils',
But delivered his sermons
In the best Queen's English.

Now forty years later
I have returned alone
To read Scottish verse
And watch other men's wives
Driving to work
In their Fiats and Cortinas.

THE ANCHORESS

I furnished carefully
The cell for my retreat:
The walls, white
And hanging on them
No representation
Of any living thing.
I took with me
Quantities
Of fresh scrolls.

But my hallucinations
Flew in and out
Of the room
On clattering wings:
Like deadly scorpions
My lusts crawled out
Of the holes in the walls.

To think I could write
Of any enlightenment
In such a place ...
(A sequel
To the scrolls of Qumran ... !)

I went back
To the fountains
And the date-palms
And the swinging camel-trains
Of the city.
And there my love
Grew rooted again
And bore fruit.

PART THREE

Relics

RELICS

It pleases me to hoard them (a few, not many)
Things that have defied the ravage of Time
As, item:
             Victorian samplers,

                          Flies in amber,
One ebony cigar-case inlaid with mother-of-pearl,
Three sets of picture cards, dated 1920,
Showing the first-ever Fokker biplane,
A water-colour, framed who knows when,
Of Highland cottages built of stone:

Hear now the gospel according to Things.

Firstly, they are modest and unassuming.

Secondly, they teach me that a thing can be loved
That serves no useful purpose.

And thirdly, they comfort me
With a kind of sombre reassurance
By their obstinate thingness,
Their dogged refusal to grow old and die.

THE VOLAPÜKISTS

The last remnant gathered on the mountain
At the hour the astrologers foretold:
'There will be rains of fire and dews of blood:
God's wrath will shrivel up a godless planet,
And after that, the dawn of Paradise'.

They waited: the hour passed.
Nothing happened: only a little rain fell.
When their food ran out, some began to mutter,
Some openly to doubt;
Then one by one, they descended from the mountain.

Some to settle again in their old homes,
Others to castigate their children
In simple vengefulness,
Others to practise the magic formula,
Which, though failed once, might work a second time ...

Since then most are gone, commemorated
By here and there a grassy mound, a plaque
In a crematorium, or a set of pamphlets
Offered at half-price by some booksellers;
But nothing can recapture
The urgency and bliss of that far-off morning
When the whole earth trembled and was still.

THREE DREAMS

1. The Husband's Dream

I'd like to go on a foolish voyage
To the edge of the known world,
If it has one — hardly so,
Civilisation expanding all the time —
A foolish voyage
Not as in former years, primped
And dry-cleaned, like any
Naïve college date,
But in duck and denims, a roll
Of tobacco in the pouch
And a store of anecdotes up my sleeve
And a spare necktie somewhere
For the odd formal occasion.
What wouldn't I see?
Peacocks and pagodas —
Pandas and princesses —
The Palace of Versailles and the Panama Canal.
I'd leave now, if it wasn't
I have this washing up to do,
A boss to please
And the wife and kids to feed.
So New York and L.A.
Are going to have to get along without me.
I call it a foolish voyage
But of course it would be
A passport to supreme wisdom,
The quintessence of all the Buddhas
Distilled into a season.
At all events, such a trip
Could not possibly be so foolish
As the one (looking back
Through twenty years of World Cup-watching,
Child-raising and commuting)
I actually took.

2. The Wife's Dream

He looks past me now, or over my shoulder,
As I look over his
At the ghosts of old lovers
Grown indistinct with the years.
Someone to care — I wanted.
Well, surely that was granted:
Thank God for the instalment plan.
I can look forward
To the customary downward ecstasies.
I paint in water-colours, who once
          painted my own face.
The expanding ripples of a single act
Are all today and summer.

3. The Child's Dream

Why in hell's name wasn't I born
Of intelligent parents? These ones
Hardly understand new math, or Algol,
Or any input since the 1900's.
Sex seems to have happened to them once,
Or I wouldn't be here — but love,
That nicest of recurring decimals
Was hardly ever rung up on their till.
To have to delay fulfilment
For another decade, and pander
To such authoritarian anti-life
It makes one puke, it does.

The Elks should win hands down next Saturday.
Zebra crossings are for old folk.
Sure Mars is inhabited! Wanna bet??

AN ARTS DEGREE

To outgrow our fifth-form notions, or to be groomed
In the attitudes appropriate to an élite?
Anyway off we were packed on the train to Oxford:
From the day we drank cool claret under the gas-jets,
To the chilly dénouement in the Examination Schools,
What remains of importance?

The one-eyed College porter dissecting bicycles,
The billowing gowns in the Turl, the mad professors
Ageless and venerable as California redwoods,
The dripping honey-cake eaten from a paper napkin,
Auden at the Cadena, the swallow's wings ...
All these have attained a sort of permanence.

Not so the containerised learning, the ponderous theses
Waiting their turn for their recyclement into pulp,
The nervousness of the young who challenge the old,
Not so the fatal indifference to the family,
And even to the claims of common humanity,
Fiddling while London burned.

I am pleased enough that chance awarded me a look
At that self-conscious world — a world of standards
Largely crumbling, and so on the counter-offensive,
Even though its writ ran nowhere beyond Carfax,
And though it brought no personal gain but two more initials
Not before but after my name.

V—J DAY

'Hat jemand etwas Neues
Zu berichten?' asked the German master,
'Has anyone anything new
To report?'
                    We fingered
Our ink-stained primers and breathed
A throaty negative.

It was '45, three years
Since Stalingrad
And a month since the Bomb.
'Hat jemand etwas Neues
Zu berichten ... ?'

Only children learning their lessons,
And men forgetting theirs.

SOFT CORN

The Cornish course is very tastefully written,
And is, not unnaturally, largely in Cornish.

As my limited knowledge does not permit
Me to speak of that, let me introduce the characters.

The protagonists are a family called Penpol
Who live in Landhewenek which is not far from Truro.

Mr Penpol is an absent-minded estate agent
Who keeps leaving his glasses in the boot of his car.

He has a wife Tamsyn who does a nice line
In free-range eggs and fishermen's sweaters.

Their daughter Morwenna is addicted to Boy George:
She has a King Charles spaniel and a topless bikini.

Their son, Wella, went berserk one Saturday
After Landhewenek's football team lost to Lanstefan.

He is in love with a dark witch called Jenyfer
Who sticks pins into clay statuettes.

There is also a butcher and a comic policeman
Whose role in the narrative is somewhat obscure.

All this is available from Dyllas Publications
At the special price of six pounds ninety-five.

There is a follow-up course in which it is revealed
Whether Mr Penpol failed his driving test,

Whether Morwenna was nicked for indecent exposure
By the comic policeman, and whether Jenyfer's victims

Died of the curse together or one by one.

PROGRAMMER

His neurons flashing
  At two millisecs
He sits limply
  At an ormolu table
Topped by a marble
  Paperweight.

Reminder: Routine
  For POSTING A LETTER.
To find stamp:
  SEARCH.
If stamp equals 12p,
  Resume SEARCH.
If stamp equals 17p,
  Extend fingers of right hand,
Put stamp on letter,
  (At 1 cm. from right top corner)
Put letter in pocket.

His wife enters the room:
His hands extend like discs
  Only floppier
Now what was I doing
  Oh yes
Still here darling we'll be late
  for the coffee morning
GO TO POST
GO TO POST
RUN

SEPTEMBER

The swallow hurries by on forked wings,
Gobhlan-gaoithe, 'oarsman of the breezes'
(But nobody now speaks Gaelic).
The Fife hills sleep still in seeming unconcern;
The days are getting shorter.

Autumn is imminent: the squirrel and hedgehog
Forage for fodder: will they have enough
When the cold time comes and ice holds
All earth in its frosty sleep?

Man seeks oblivion: in houses lit by electricity,
Tries to defy the darkness and the rigour;
But we too own the absolute suzerainty of Time,
All we have been, thought, dreamed about
Must vanish, be postponed

To another reincarnation, another *Kalpa,*
And what conceivable reincarnation can there be
For the swallow in flight, the Fife hills
Eroding into the estuary, all the grandeur
And calm of autumn's passing, unless
Perpetuated by The Eternal Mind?

Cease to cling to illusion, accept
The death of all things, the slow invasion
Of winter, the leaf's falling, seek
Only the reconciliation of the Impermanent
With the timeless revelation
Where the world shall be transcended
And all shall be made one.

LA GRAND' PLACE, BRUSSELS

Arriving from London overnight
You took the room they offered you
On the fourth floor, underneath the clock
That dominated the town square
Ticking away the enormous hours.
You hoarded in your purse your last sixty francs
Because your allowance had not come.
All morning you sat and wondered:
'What is to be done? What will happen now?'
But your brain could admit no answer, save the sound
From stalls where garlic-sellers cried their wares
And the heavy echoes came spiralling upward.
Then at noon, the weather changed
To a sudden thunder-clap and fall of rain.
You walked as far as the Osterparkplein
Watching the raindrops glance off the empty cafe-tables.
Someone tried to ogle you from a car
But you mingled quickly with a cinema queue ...
Having no money, you could not get in.
The evening papers announced
Sixty thousand admissions to L'Expo ...
Language riots in Louvain ...
A new wing opened at Antwerp Zoo.
That was one day that never was;
But all the time
Even then your body was ripening,
Ripening surely towards some fateful action.

BACHELOR

These mid-June days are idle and unglamorous:
Out in the rain, I buy a new hearth-rug.
It has a pattern like the Hebrew letter *Shin*:
That could be a Cabbalistic symbol
For something exciting, a birth, a housewarming.

Distracted I potter around the kitchen,
Upset a carton of milk, suddenly remember
That what I am wanting is someone like you
To dispense forgiveness for my unwary acts.

Who am I talking to? There's nobody here
After all. I must be dreaming.
Out in the street the sound of heavy lorries
Dwindles to a scarcely audible clamour.

LA BAULE IN AUTUMN

In mid-September, the hectic fever subsided
Of the tearaways on mopeds, the tourists in mindless droves,
Quietly, determinedly, and without presumption,
The artists once again return to the scene
Of their chosen tasks, which are never completed
Because they are always imposing new demands,
Of rendering, one in ink and one in oils
And one in melody, Goodness, Truth and Beauty.

They do not take Dame Nature by storm.
They have not fathered millions of starving children.
They do not manufacture useless gadgets
To sell to the bored inhabitants of cities.
They have not seen their natural curiosity
Eroded by Time to mere familiarity.
Alone they have kept the faith.

No wonder the *Mairie* is glad to see them!
The gendarme salutes and smilingly pockets the summons:
The pigeons are pleased with the crumbs they scatter
Under the palm-trees, and the estranging sea
Explodes in endless hosannas to their honour.